Feelings

Copyright © 1980, Raintree Publishers Inc.

All rights reserved. No part of this book may be
reproduced or utilized in any form or by any means,
electronic or mechanical, including photocopying,
recording, or by any information storage and retrieval
system, without permission in writing from the Publisher.
Inquiries should be addressed to Raintree Childrens Books.
330 East Kilbourn Avenue, Milwaukee, Wisconsin 53202

Library of Congress Number: 79-27549

    6 7 8 9 0 88 87 86 85

Printed in the United States of America.

Library of Congress Cataloging in Publication Data

Allington, Richard L
  Feelings.

  (Beginning to learn about)
  SUMMARY: Presents situations arousing such common
feelings as anger, embarrassment, bravery, pride and
surprise. Includes related activities.
  I. Emotions — Juvenile literature. [1. Emotions]
I. Cowles, Kathleen, joint author. II. Cody, Brian.
III. Title. IV. Series.
BF561.A48   152.4   79-27549

Richard L. Allington is Associate Professor, Department of Reading,
State University of New York at Albany.
Kathleen Cowles is the author of several picture books.

BEGINNING TO LEARN ABOUT

FEELINGS

BY RICHARD L. ALLINGTON, PH.D., • AND KATHLEEN COWLES

ILLUSTRATED BY BRIAN CODY

Raintree Childrens Books • Milwaukee • Toronto • Melbourne • London

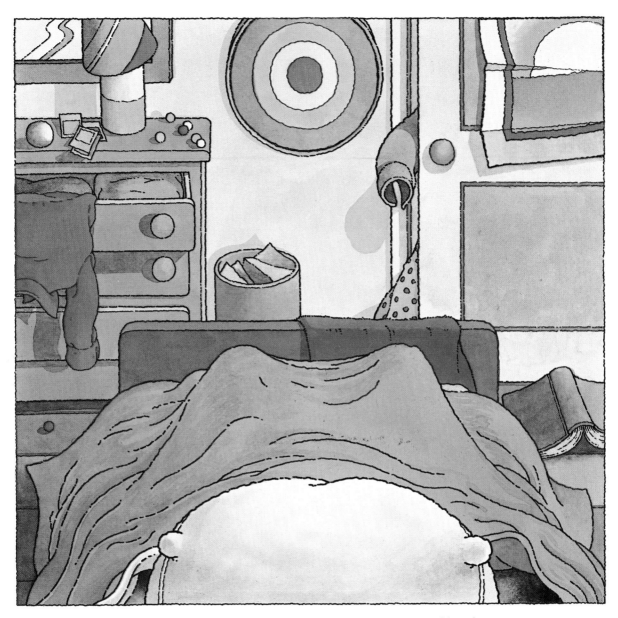

First thing this morning, my mom yelled at me
for having a messy room. I wanted
to tell her that I *liked* it that way.

I was **mad**.

Before I could say anything,
my dog came running into my room.
He landed right on top of me.

I felt **helpless**.

My mom got the dog off of me.
I cleaned up my room. Then I took
a shower. It felt good.

I was **wide-awake**.

My dad and I went jogging to the park
and back. Then we had a big breakfast.

We felt **healthy**.

It was time to go to school.
I walked there with the new kid next door.
She has a big dog too.

I felt **friendly**.

Just as we walked in to school, I tripped on the stairs. The other kids saw me.

I was **embarrassed**.

My first class was math. The teacher
asked questions. Everyone but me
knew the answers.

I felt **confused**.

In art class, the teacher asked kids
to show their paintings to the class.
I decided to show mine.

I felt **brave**.

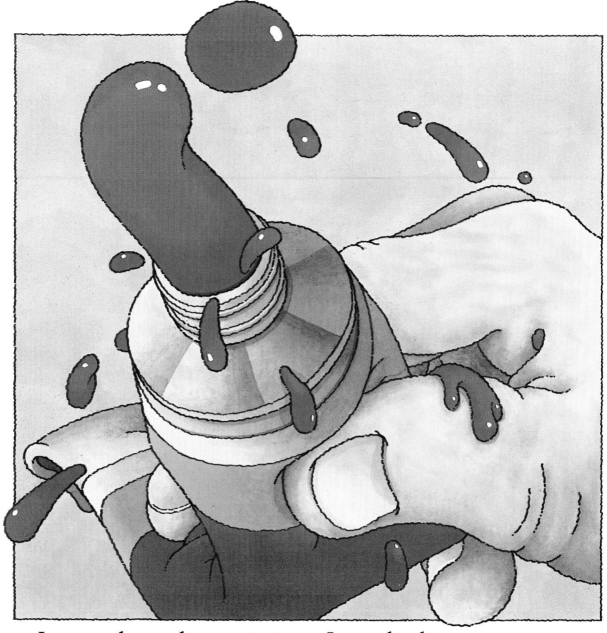

I started another painting. I reached
for my red paint. It kept squirting
all over my clothes.

I felt **frustrated**.

 At lunchtime, all the other kids
had candy and cupcakes for dessert.
All I had was an apple.

I felt **jealous**.

When I bit into my apple, I found
a worm in it.

I felt **sick**.

Out on the playground, I told some of
my friends a joke. We laughed so hard
that we couldn't stop for a long time.

We felt **silly**.

Then my friends played a game.
I didn't know how to play.

I felt **shy**.

I tried to play the game anyway.
I overheard some kid telling another kid
that my feet were big.

I felt **unfriendly**.

In science class we talked about machines like robots and spaceships.

I was **curious**.

My last class of the day was reading.
I already know how to read. The book was
too easy.

I felt **bored**.

After school, I went to the toy store.
I got to buy anything I wanted
with the money I earned last weekend.

I felt **happy**.

On the way home, I turned
the wrong way by mistake.

For a while I felt **lost**.

Finally I found the right way home.
My mom and dad were still at work.
My brother wasn't home yet either.

I felt **lonely**.

   While I waited for someone to come home,
I washed the breakfast dishes.
But I put too much soap in the sink.

I was **worried**.

I cleaned up the mess. No one was
home yet. I decided to read one
of my brother's books. It was hard.

I felt **proud**.

Then I set the book down. I didn't see
my brother's glasses until it was too late.

I felt **sorry**.

At dinner, my brother said
that those were old glasses. And my mom
and dad thanked me for doing the dishes.
They made pizza for dinner.

I felt **glad**.

After dinner we all worked on a jigsaw puzzle.
I put in the most pieces.

I felt **clever**.

Then we went to see a scary movie.

I felt **afraid**.

I stayed up past my bedtime to watch TV.

I felt **sleepy**.

I went to bed. I found out that my dog
was already there.

I was **surprised**.

I chased my dog out of my bed. I got
under the covers and started to dream.
It was nice and warm in my bed.

I felt **safe**.

Tell someone about the last time you felt some of the feelings that the person in this book did. What words would you use to tell about your feelings?

Some of the words that we use to tell about feelings are opposites. With your finger, draw a line from each word to its opposite.

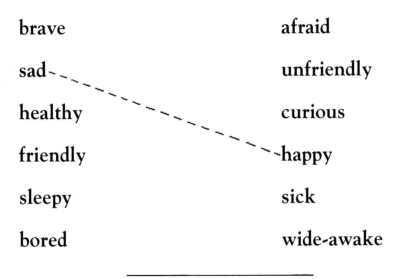

brave   afraid

sad   unfriendly

healthy   curious

friendly   happy

sleepy   sick

bored   wide-awake

Make your own book about feelings. Look through a newspaper or magazine. Find pictures of people. Cut out the pictures. Tape or paste them onto pieces of paper. Then write down a word that tells what feeling each person has. Fasten the papers together. You may ask an adult to help you.